THE APPRAISAL WRITING HANDBOOK

BY

ALAN BLANKENSHIP, PH.D.

APPRAISAL INSTITUTE®

875 North Michigan Avenue
Chicago, Illinois 60611-1980

www.appraisalinstitute.org

Reviewers:	Thomas Markley, SRA
	Thomas A. Motta, MAI, SRA
	Janice F. Young, MAI, RM

Senior Vice President, Communications:	Christopher Bettin
Manager, Book Development:	Michael R. Milgrim, PhD
Senior Editor:	Stephanie Shea-Joyce
Manager, Design/Production:	Julie B. Beich
Graphic Designer:	Claire Krzyzewski

For Educational Purposes Only

The material presented in this text has been reviewed by members of the Appraisal Institute, but the opinions and procedures set forth by the author are not necessarily endorsed as the only methodology consistent with proper appraisal practice. While a great deal of care has been taken to provide accurate and current information, neither the Appraisal Institute nor its editors and staff assume responsibility for the accuracy of the data contained herein. Further, the general principles and conclusions presented in this text are subject to local, state, and federal laws and regulations, court cases, and any revisions of the same. This publication is sold for educational purposes with the understanding that the publisher is not engaged in rendering legal, accounting, or other professional service.

Nondiscrimination Policy

The Appraisal Institute advocates equal opportunity and nondiscrimination in the appraisal profession and conducts its activities in accordance with applicable federal, state, and local laws.

Printed in the United States of America

02   01   00   99   98   5   4   3   2   1

Library of Congress Cataloging-in-Publication Data
Blankenship, Alan.
    The appraisal writing handbook / by Alan Blankenship.
        p.   cm.
    ISBN 0-922154-46-5
    1. Real estate—Valuation.   2. Business writing.   I. Title.
HD1387.B538   1997
333.33'2—dc21
                                       97-49263
                                           CIP

CONTENTS

Foreword v

Introduction vii

Chapter 1   Basics of Appraisal Writing 1

Chapter 2   Visual Aspects of the Report 4

Chapter 3   Developing a Persuasive Reporting Style 16

Chapter 4   Selling the Value Conclusion 26

Chapter 5   Achieving Correctness in Appraisal Reports 32

Chapter 6   Punctuation Guide 42

Chapter 7   Documentation 48

Chapter 8   Editing and Proofreading 51

ABOUT THE AUTHOR

Alan L. Blankenship, PhD, is an independent writing consultant who has extensive experience in educating business professionals. He specializes in appraisal report writing and has taught and developed courses and seminars for the Appraisal Institute as well as other business, industry, and governmental organizations. Blankenship has a master's degree in English from the University of Virginia in Charlottesville and a PhD from the University of Colorado in Boulder. He currently resides in Boulder, Colorado, and can be reached at (303) 494-7251.

FOREWORD

To the client, the appraisal report is the tangible result of the valuation process. Whether the appraisal is communicated in a self-contained narrative report or on a form, it is a persuasive document that informs and educates the reader about a particular piece of property. Therefore, it is imperative that appraisers work to develop a logical, fluent writing style that effectively communicates their analyses and conclusions to their clients.

The Appraisal Writing Handbook is a guide to written composition designed for the special requirements of the appraisal profession. Beginning with writing basics and the visual aspects of an appraisal report, it demonstrates how an appraiser can develop a concise reporting style that will reveal the significance of the data presented in the report and convince readers of the correctness of the appraiser's conclusions.

This handbook offers practical tips to help appraisers achieve effective communication and avoid common writing pitfalls. Readers will learn how to write reports that are interesting and readable as well as logical, well-organized, accurate, and well-documented. Although no one reporting style is right for all assignments or all appraisers, the text offers solutions to many writing problems appraisers face.

Appraisers write detailed appraisal reports on a regular basis and all practitioners can endeavor to become more comfortable, and more proficient, at this crucial task.

Joseph R. Stanfield, Jr., MAI, SRA
1998 President
Appraisal Institute

INTRODUCTION

Few people choose to become appraisers primarily because it provides an opportunity to write lengthy, detailed reports on a regular, sometimes daily, basis. Nevertheless, almost no group of professionals, except lawyers, is required to write more than appraisers. Rising to this challenge, the appraisal profession has demonstrated a serious commitment to the rigors of careful and exact communication. Standard 2 of the Uniform Standards of Professional Appraisal Practice (USPAP) requires appraisers to communicate their appraisals clearly, and there is a very real desire among appraisers to improve the whole reporting process.

Information on the required content of appraisal reports can be obtained from numerous sources. *The Appraisal of Real Estate,* eleventh edition, includes a detailed discussion of the contents of a self-contained report, and the Appraisal Institute's Courses 540 and 500 address this type of report in great depth. The content requirements for summary and form reports are also covered in many Appraisal Institute publications. This handbook does not attempt to duplicate this material, but instead focuses on writing style, reporting techniques, and selecting a format that effectively communicates information to the client. This is a writing handbook designed for the special requirements of the appraisal profession.

Report writers should keep in mind that the appraisal report is a persuasive document. The reporting process is quite separate from the appraisal process. In performing the valuation, the appraiser tries to discover the truth objectively and to arrive at a conclusion about value. The appraiser does not know the answer until the process is complete. The reporting process, however, begins with the answer, and the appraiser's task is to convey the value conclusion persuasively and clearly to a client, while at the same time fulfilling all professional requirements.

No one can produce an appraisal report without facing a multitude of decisions about the appearance of the report, the level of formality to employ in the writing style, and the amount of data and explanation to provide. Every appraisal report demonstrates the individual writer's decisions about what contributes to an effective report and what is required in the reporting process. Any reviewer of appraisal reports recognizes that a remarkable variety in reporting styles are used by practitioners and that some styles are more effective than others.

While no single reporting style is right for everyone, this handbook takes a stand on many of the writing issues facing appraisers. The most important criterion is, does it work? Does it convey the appraisal analysis and conclusions effectively and persuasively so that a client can follow the narrative and have confidence in the findings? While some of the advice presented here is clearly a matter of opinion— and a few appraisers may disagree with it —none of the information in this text contradicts the Appraisal Institute's teachings, specifically the material in Courses 540 and 500.

Chapter 1 provides an overview of major concerns relating to appraisal reporting. The next chapter deals with the visual aspects of the report, focusing on organization and layout techniques. Computers provide so many formatting options that writers may agonize over the numerous decisions required. However, desktop publishing experts can offer much advice to help appraisers create a document that is both readable and reader-friendly. This chapter also discusses graphic elements, which communicate powerfully when they are presented properly in a report. Chapters 3 and 4 pertain to word choice and persuasive reporting techniques, which will help make the narrative more concise and readable and the conclusions more convincing.

Chapter 5 answers frequently asked questions on grammar and number presentation, and Chapter 6 is a quick guide to correct punctuation. Chapter 7 discusses effective methods for documenting sources in a report, and Chapter 8 addresses the final steps in the reporting process, editing and proofreading for clarity and correctness.

This handbook is the result of 10 years of work with thousands of practicing appraisers. The experience has given me immense respect for these professionals, who face many challenges in creating effective reports and have demonstrated an ongoing effort to produce honest, ethical reports and improve their communication with the public. These are noble goals and I hope that this handbook can be of some use in achieving them.

CHAPTER 1

Basics of Appraisal Writing

CONSIDER THE READER.

The value of any communication depends solely on the response it produces in the reader.

In preparing an appraisal report, the writer's most important concern is maintaining a sense of reader awareness. No communication succeeds unless the reader can follow and understand the writing. Ultimately, it is the reader or client who determines the success of communication. If the client is confused, overwhelmed, or bored, the writer is to blame. This may seem to place a heavy responsibility on appraisers, given the complexity of the appraisal process, the rather arcane nature of many appraisal procedures, and the impatience some readers have with long reports. However, the first step in overcoming these hurdles is to write with a clear concern for what the reader needs and wants to know.

Assessing the audience's response is much easier in oral communication. The listener's body language, facial expressions, and questions clearly indicate when the speaker needs to slow down, speed up, or clarify something. Written communication is a much more difficult task, however, because it is impossible to monitor the reader's response. Instead, the writer must make certain assumptions about the reader and anticipate potential misunderstandings.

Identifying the needs and desires of the reader is often easy when writing business letters, memos, professional articles, or in-house reports. The writer often knows the specific reader's educational background, level of experience, business needs, and particular interests. An appraiser's job is more difficult, however, because an appraisal report can end up almost anywhere. It is difficult for the writer to match the level of language to a particular audience. Clients can differ immensely in background and may include lay readers, lawyers, bankers, investors, and professional review appraisers.

Determining the proper level of communication is difficult when the potential audience is varied in background and experience. One key is to think about the use of the appraisal. The readers of appraisal reports used for refinancing, tax appeal, and large portfolio valuation usually differ. Using the same reporting style for all occasions will guarantee poor communication, an ineffective report, and probably an unhappy client.

STRIVE FOR CLARITY IN WRITING.

Amateurs complicate; professionals simplify.
Thought may be circular, amorphous, and repetitious, but writing must be linear. The writer must hammer a logical sequence out of rather shapeless thoughts. Good writing is the product of good thinking, which requires sifting out irrelevant ideas, focusing on the goal, and creating a logical progression so the writing makes sense to the reader.

The appraiser's goal is to communicate the appraisal process in such a way that the client can follow the logic and not misunderstand or be confused. The general structure of most appraisal reports (as fully described in *The Appraisal of Real Estate*) is a logical, four-part framework, but unfortunately not all clients are familiar with this standard design. The writer needs to communicate how the various parts of the report fit together and lead ultimately to the final estimate of value.

Not only must the writer reveal the clarity of the overall plan, but he or she must also strive for clarity in each individual sections. How, for example, were the adjustments derived? Why was the upper end of the range selected? Why is Sale 3's location superior to the subject? A typical appraisal uncovers so many potential questions that answering them all can become an overwhelming task. It would be easy to bewilder the reader with too much information, for theoretically *everything* affects value.

To address this problem, many people fall back on the acronym KISS (keep it simple, stupid), but that axiom misses the point. The real task is to create a sense of simplicity out of very complex information. The ability to separate the significant from the unimportant, to establish priorities in the available data, and to reveal patterns and logical sequences are all skills that lead to good appraisal reporting. A good appraisal report has simplicity because the writer was able to make a complicated process appear simple.

CORRECTNESS IS VITAL.

Clients pay for accuracy and have the right to expect it.
All too often, an appraiser does careful research, prepares a thoughtful and sophisticated analysis, and then weakens the persuasiveness of the final conclusion with careless inaccuracies in the final report. To the client the report, not the hours of research, is the appraisal. The report's

accuracy is a direct reflection of the professionalism of the research and analysis. Consequently, proofreading the final document to eliminate errors in numbers, data, and writing is an integral and obligatory part of the appraisal process. The final document stands as a permanent record of the whole appraisal assignment.

While incorrect data and numbers create the substantive problems in a report, errors in grammar, sentence structure, and spelling detract subtly from the professionalism of the analysis. For a detailed discussion of the proofreading process, see Chapter 8 of this handbook.

BE CONCISE.

Take the time to make it short.
Producing a report that is succinct, yet thorough, takes much more thought and careful editing than preparing a long, rambling report. Long, theoretical introductions on various approaches and valuation procedures are readily available to anyone who wants to use them. Similarly, any chamber of commerce can provide an appraiser with tomes of data about a region and city. Using such material will "bulk up" an appraisal report, but is that necessary? Many clients would respond with a vehement "no." In fact, the recent popularity of summary reports is, in part, a reaction against voluminous reports full of information and verbiage that clients neither need nor want to read.

To be effective, an appraisal report must be read, and that means appraisers must do everything possible to keep reports concise. Few clients have the time or inclination to wade through reading material that is not clearly relevant and useful. Writers must constantly ask themselves, "Is this information or explanation truly necessary and relevant? Does it directly affect the conclusions about use and value set forth in the report?" If the answer is "no," the material should not be included in the report. Eliminating material that does not move the reader one step closer to understanding the report conclusions will shorten a report and make it more focused. The result will be a report that the client will read and understand.

Visual Aspects of the Report

As noted previously, the appraisal report constitutes the whole appraisal from the client's point of view. It represents all the hours of research, field work, and analysis that have gone into the complete appraisal assignment. The report document is a permanent record and its presentation is very important. The reader responds to the way it looks, its organization, and its layout; these characteristics establishes a powerful first impression. Long ago, Marshall McLuhan commented that the media speaks as loudly as the message. The appearance of an appraisal report speaks forcefully to the reader even before it is read.

Few appraisers believe that every reader, every client, reads a report from cover to cover. Some do read carefully, of course, but many only peruse the report, dipping into sections of particular interest. Lack of time is probably the most common reason clients don't read reports completely, but the massive length of some reports and the bewildering density of others may dissuade many clients. Even readers who only peruse reports will come away with a positive or negative impression of how professional and credible the report and the value estimate are.

Ideally the writer will create a document that is readable and attractive, one that asks to be read simply because it is clearly organized and well presented. Inviting visual elements and a logical page layout demonstrate that the appraiser is making every effort to communicate clearly, concisely, and simply. Creating such a document is easy given the capabilities of today's computers, laser printers, and software programs for word processing, desktop publishing, and graphics. The abundance of new possibilities has created another problem for writers. How does one choose among all the available fonts, text sizes, page layouts, and graphing capabilities? This chapter will discuss how desktop publishing techniques can be used to organize a report effectively for a general reading audience.

CLARIFY THE ORGANIZATION.

The Uniform Standards do not require a specific organizational structure for appraisal reports, but tradition and experience have made the four-part structure shown below the accepted norm. This outline is taken from, and explained in, *The Appraisal of Real Estate,* eleventh edition.

Part One—Introduction
Title page
Letter of transmittal
Table of contents
Certification of value
Summary of important conclusions

Part Two—Premises of the Appraisal
Identification of type of appraisal and report format
Assumptions and limiting conditions
Purpose and use of the appraisal
Definition of value and date of value estimate
Property rights appraised
Scope of the appraisal (the process of collecting, confirming, and
    reporting data)

Part Three—Presentation of Data
Identification of the property, legal description
Identification of any personal property or other items
    that are not real property
Area, city, neighborhood, and location data
Site data
Description of improvements
Zoning
Taxes and assessment data
History, including prior sales and current offers or listings
Marketability study, if appropriate

Part Four—Analysis of Data and Conclusions
Highest and best use of the land as though vacant
Highest and best use of the property as improved
Site value
Cost approach
Sales comparison approach
Income capitalization approach
Reconciliation and final value estimate
Estimate of marketing period
Qualifications of the appraiser

A typical reader might look at this list of topics and ask, "Why must I wade through 75% of the report before I come to the meat, which is the analysis?" Although this question may seem naive to appraisers, they should remember that an appraisal report is unfamiliar territory for many readers.

For many, Part Two—Premises of the Appraisal is the great stumbling block. The definitions and limiting conditions presented may appear irrelevant and confusing to the lay reader. By clearly identifying this section as *premises of the appraisal* and explaining that all the subsequent analysis and conclusions depend on these qualifications and definitions, the writer indicates the significance of these pages.

Part Three—Presentation of Data appears more directly related to the estimate of value, but readers can become lost here too if voluminous boilerplate is presented in the descriptions of the region and city. The writer can keep the reader's attention by periodically mentioning how the region and city data and analysis relate to the subject property and to its use and value. If no direct relationship can be demonstrated, the data could probably be eliminated from the report.

Part Four—Analysis of Data and Conclusions describes several, fairly standardized processes. The four tests commonly used to determine highest and best use (legal permissibility, physical possibility, financial feasibility, and maximal productivity) provide a general reporting structure for this crucial part of the report. Similarly, each of the three approaches to value involves application of a logical procedure, which provides an ordered sequence for these sections. Although Part Four is, or should be, the longest section of the report, it may well be the easiest to organize because it describes step-by-step processes.

It is important to remember that the logical structure of an appraisal report is not self-evident to general readers. The writer must constantly highlight that structure and show how the various parts of the report fit together.

REVEAL THE ORGANIZATION VISUALLY.

The easiest way to communicate long, complex subject matter is to break it into small, easily digested parts, a process call "chunking." Each of these smaller sections requires a heading, subheadings, and possibly sub-subheadings, which reveal the overall organization of the report visually. Some parts of the report lend themselves to "chunking" simply because they are lists of data or definitions. The approaches to value can easily be broken down into logical steps for the reader to follow. For other sections, like the descriptions of the neighborhood, region, and city, the writer can create meaningful subheadings that indicate the content of the discussion. These subheadings help readers find information quickly and they break up long sections of narrative with white space. As a rule, every page in an appraisal report should have at least one heading or subheading per page.

There are many systems for creating headings and subheadings, and none is more correct that the others. Writers are free to use a variety of methods to distinguish headings from sub-headings and sub-subheadings, including any logical combination of the following:

- placement on the page (centered or aligned at the left)
- type size
- change in type font
- capitalization
- boldface type

The writer must devise a system that is logical and predictable and use headings liberally to guide the reader through the report.

USE DESKTOP PUBLISHING TECHNIQUES TO INCREASE READABILITY.

By now, most offices have abandoned their typewriters for computers and it is time to abandon the typewriter mentality about page layout as well. Before computers and laser printers, writers had few options. Typewriters could be used to print capital or lowercase letters, underline, indent, and (after much calculating) center type. The only readily available typeface was Courier type. Today all that has changed and the layout choices now facing writers are almost overwhelming. The following suggestions have been gleaned from various desktop publishing sources.

Typeface. Choose a serif font for basic text. All printer fonts fall into two general categories: serif and sans serif. A serif font has a tiny tail, or serif, at the end of each stroke in a letter; a sans serif font does not.

This is a sample of a serif font.

This is a sample of a sans serif font.

Notice how the serifs at the bottom of the letters indicate a baseline for the type. This baseline helps to ground the line of print and make it more readable. Because of its readability, most books and textbooks are printed in serif fonts. Perhaps the most common serif font is Times Roman or one of its many variants.

A sans serif font may be used for headings, titles, tables, or graphics, however, because this text does not involve extended reading. For appraisal reports, one should avoid any font that is **cute** (Regular Joe), *fancy* (Park Avenue) or **illegible** (Blackoak). Finally, do not use too many fonts or the report will appear amateurish.

Size. Choose 10- or 12-point type for the body of the report. Headings can be larger, but the text of the report should be no smaller than 10 point and no larger than 12 point. Larger or smaller type tends to be too hard to read comfortably. Sometimes quoted passages are set in smaller type, but anything much smaller than 10 point tells the reader, "I don't expect (or want) you to read this."

Line length. Shorter lines are more readable. The traditional appraisal report is printed on 8.5-by-11-in. paper with one-inch margins, producing a 6.5-in. line of print. By comparison, most books have lines 4.5 inches long or less and newspapers and magazines use even shorter lines. Publishers know that a shorter line is more readable.

To increase the readability of an appraisal report, the writer might increase the margins from one to one and one-half inches or consider indenting subsections of the report. Creating a shorter line is particular important for passages containing many numbers, dense subject matter, or technical language.

Recently, many appraisers have experimented with a two-column format, with section headings in a narrow left column and the text in the wider right column. This can result in a much more readable report with more white space and shorter, more legible lines of print. Surprisingly, shortening the line length need not increase the length of the report. Instead the preparer can tighten the line spacing and reduce the font size, which will not decrease readability when a short line of print is used.

Justification. Full justification can produce a visually boring report because every paragraph becomes a gray rectangle. Moreover, a uniform right margin decreases readability as the eye moves down the page and encounters no variation in shape. A more ragged right margin is especially important when text is set in a full, 6.5-in. line. With shorter lines, the eye is less likely to lose its place.

In spite of its reduced legibility, some (but not most) authorities still suggest full justification for formal reports. However, virtually all agree that letters, memos, and other, less formal communication should not be fully justified.

Creating emphasis. Avoid using underlining and all capital letters for emphasis. Underlining has long been used by editors and proofreaders to indicate that text should be set in italics. Underlining was one of the few emphasizing techniques available when typewriters were used, but today report writers have better options. Similarly, using capitals for emphasis was common in the age of typewriters. Unfortunately, ALL CAPS MAKES EVERY WORD HAVE THE SAME SHAPE, a small rectangle. Because word shape facilitates reading, sentences in capital letters are harder to read. Design experts suggest that writers abandon underlining and capitalization as means of emphasis.

Computers have made it possible for writers to use methods of emphasis—boldface, italics, larger font size—that were previously only available to publishers. Creating white space around a word or phrase is another way to draw the reader's attention to it. All of these options are preferable to underlining and capitalization. Writers must remember, however, that any attention-grabbing device loses its punch if used too frequently.

The Appraisal Writing Handbook

GRAPHICS ARE POWERFUL REPORTING TOOLS.

Appraisal reports are full of numbers and raw data, most of which are more familiar and meaningful to the appraiser than the client. The conclusions in an appraisal depend on the clear, persuasive presentation of numbers and data. One powerful tool for presenting information is a graphic, which can be easily created by computer.

As a rule, numbers and words do not mix well in a paragraph. Most readers have a very low tolerance for numbers embedded in prose, as the following passage illustrates.

> New housing starts in both the county and city have varied in the last 10 years. In 1987, the city saw 782 starts, and the county 408. The following year, however, the numbers rose to 917 in the city and 644 in the county. During the next three years the levels remained very similar; the city had 893, 924, and 905, and the county had 656, 632, and 648. Lower interest rates probably account for the marked rise during 1992 and 1993, for the city had 1,143 and 1,264, while the county had 877 and 934. The last three years have seen a gradual decline in the number of housing starts, the city having 1,241, 1,224, and 1,197 in 1994,1995, and 1996, respectively. The county had 928, 918, and 905 in those same years.

While this passage is an exaggeration, it illustrates how difficult it is to comprehend statistics when they are not presented graphically. A simple table could be used to present these figures more meaningfully or, if the individual numbers are not terribly significant, a line graph like the one shown in Exhibit 1 could be included to show the trend in building starts.

The graph reveals the trends immediately and powerfully. The picture makes the point, and the reader does not need to struggle with the raw data and risk deriving an erroneous conclusion. Once the data is presented in a "picture," the writer can use prose to discuss and interpret the data. Narrative discussion of the graphic display is vital so the writer can tell the reader what is significant about the information displayed.

The graphic and the text are interconnected. No graphic should appear in a report until it has been referenced. The writer tells the reader the graphic is going to appear and then explains what it means or demonstrates. If the table or figure is well labeled, the data need not be repeated in the text, but the reader should not be left to interpret the information alone. The writer should identify trends, draw conclusions, and integrate these conclusions into the general discussion.

CALCULATIONS NEED TO BE SURROUNDED BY WHITE SPACE.

Following the steps in a calculation is much easier if the numbers are broken out from the text and separated with white space. A small, clearly

Exhibit 1. Housing Starts in City and County, 1987-1996

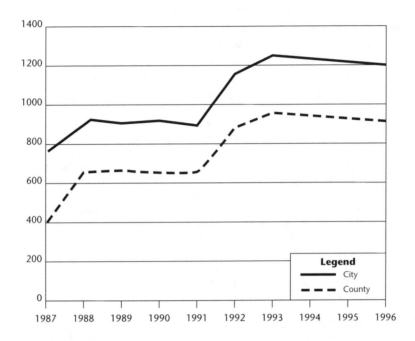

labeled table makes calculations easier to understand. Instead of describing a calculation as follows:

> Sale 2 sold in May 1996 for $675,000 and resold in July 1997 for $710,000, which shows an increase of $35,000 in 14 months. The $35,000 difference divided by $675,000 indicates 5.2% appreciation in 14 months, or 0.4% a month.

the writer could include the following statement and table:

> The sale and resale of Sale 2 indicates an appreciation rate of 0.4% per month, as shown below:

	Date Sold	Price
Sale 2	July 1997	$710,000
Sale 2	May 1996	675,000
Difference	14 months	$ 35,000

$35,000 / $675,000 = 5.2% increase in 14 months, or 0.4% per month

USE TABLES AND SPREADSHEETS EFFECTIVELY.

Appraisal reports depend on tables and spreadsheets more than other types of graphics. Usually tables set forth numbers or other data in columns or show a series of simultaneous calculations, as in a sales adjustment grid. A clearly identified table with carefully labeled data is an excellent way to present information that would be very cumbersome to narrate.

There is a danger, however, in the overwhelming size of some tables. Readers can become discouraged or confused when confronted with masses of numbers or data, even if they are clearly labeled. A writer should always ask: What is this table trying to convey? What is the point? The best tables are analytical in that they do more than simply show data. For example, a summary table of comparable sales is presented to identify differences that must be addressed in the adjustment process. The sales descriptions give facts about each sale, but the summary table arrays the data so the client can see how the sales compare to the subject. The appraiser does not list everything he or she knows about each sale but, instead, presents only the elements of comparison that significantly affect sale prices. The table provides a bridge between the raw data and the analysis performed in the adjustment process.

Like any spreadsheet, an adjustment grid displays simultaneous calculations. The adjusted sale prices derived for the comparable sales need to be mathematically demonstrated for the table to be convincing. Moreover, the derivation or basis for every number in the table should be discussed in the narrative. Without clear explanation and justification, the numbers remain mysterious to the client and the table produces more questions than answers. Sales characteristics that cannot be adjusted for mathematically should be considered in the reconciliation process. The impact of these nonquantifiable differences can provide meaningful support for the selection of a particular point in the range of adjusted sale prices.

Readers often look at tables and other exhibits (maps, graphs, photographs) out of context. While browsing through a document, readers tend to pause at the graphics. Consequently, it is imperative that the writer provide clear titles and meaningful abbreviations and acronyms. If space is limited, consider explaining unusual terms in footnotes to the tables. Try to anticipate any questions that readers may have about the data in a table and provide answers in advance. For example, a footnote might be used to explain that a sale price shown in the table includes a deduction for personal property and is not the actual sale price shown in the sale write-up. Ideally graphics ought to communicate without any accompanying narrative, but sometimes an explanatory note is needed.

PIE CHARTS, LINE GRAPHS, AND BAR GRAPHS REVEAL RELATIONSHIPS AND TRENDS.

While tables focus the reader's attention on precise numbers, often the appraiser wants to demonstrate important relationships between the figures or to show trends in the data. In fact, many important conclusions in appraisals are based on observed trends and relationships. Demonstrating these observations to a client with a table may be difficult, however, because the precision of the numbers can distract the reader. In such instances, line graphs, pie charts, and bar graphs can be excellent communication tools. These graphs are extremely powerful and persuasive. Each type of graph has a special use and is best used to highlight a specific kind of relationship.

Pie charts are an excellent way to illustrate the relative portions of a whole. For example, a small pie chart could be used to show land-use patterns in a neighborhood description. Most clients do not need numerical specificity about land use, but they do want a general impression, which a pie chart reveals vividly and quickly (see Exhibit 2).

Exhibit 2. Land Use in North End Neighborhood

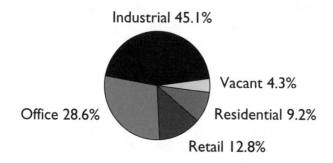

Industrial 45.1%

Vacant 4.3%

Office 28.6%

Residential 9.2%

Retail 12.8%

Line graphs plot the intersection of points on two axes— X, the horizontal axis, and Y, the vertical axis. The points of intersection may be connected to show trends, interpreted with a least squares or regression line, or left unconnected to show the absence of a clear trend. Each type of line graph illustrates a relationship. Exhibit 3 shows a graph of land sales over time with a regression line. The constant, which in this case is date of sale (time), should always appear on the horizontal axis; the variable (price per square foot) appears on the vertical axis.

Exhibit 3. Land Sales Over Time

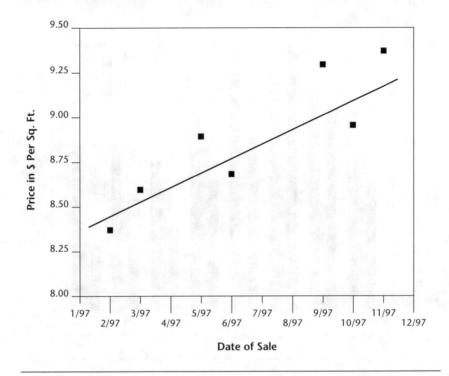

The minimum and maximum values shown on the vertical axis can radically change the shape of the graph and the impression it makes. A wide difference between minimum and maximum values flattens the regression line, suggesting less change, and a small difference exaggerates the amount of change. Changing the minimum and maximum values can easily distort the picture.

Bar graphs, like line graphs, make use of a vertical and a horizontal axis, but they can often reveal more complicated relationships. For example, a bar graph can be used to track changing relationships over time. Exhibit 4 shows vacancies for three classes of office buildings over a seven-year period.

PLACE GRAPHICS AND EXHIBITS WHERE THEY COMMUNICATE MOST EFFECTIVELY.

Deciding where to place an exhibit or graphic in a report depends on its function. Is the exhibit merely recording data to verify that research was performed? Is it demonstrating a trend required to draw a conclusion in the report? Is it calculating a crucial value? If the reader needs to see the exhibit to believe the conclusion, then it should be in the body of the report. Do not force clients to search through the addenda for vital

Exhibit 4. Vacancy Rates for Class A, B, and C Office Buildings

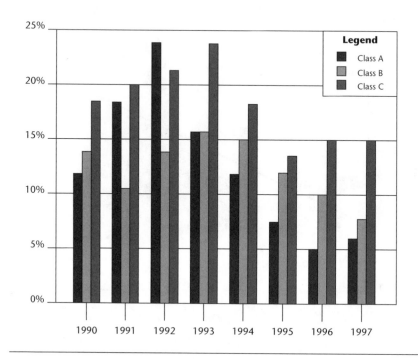

information. While the addenda are technically part of the report, they are the least effective place to put necessary information. Readers typically infer that the addenda contain only additional, nonessential information.

Small exhibits will not disrupt the body of the report. In fact, many software programs allow the text to flow around small graphics. Some writers fear that full-page tables and graphs will interrupt the flow of the report. An occasional, full-page exhibit on a left-side, facing page rarely disrupts the flow of the narrative and allows the reader to refer to the displayed data while reading the explanatory text on the right. A map showing neighborhood boundaries, for example, works well on the page facing the narrative discussion of the neighborhood. Placing summary tables and adjustment grids on facing pages gives the reader immediate access to the data discussed in the narrative and makes it easier for the reader to follow the analysis.

LABEL AND NUMBER EXHIBITS FOR EASY REFERENCE.

Exhibit titles and labels are important for the sake of clarity and to help readers, who often look at graphic elements out of context. In fact, logical labels can often guide a reader through the steps in a complicated table so that a detailed narrative explanation is not needed. Narrative explanations are often difficult to write and to follow; step-by-step headings in tables are usually clearer.

While every exhibit must have a title, numbering the exhibits is optional. Nevertheless, numbers make it easy to refer to an exhibit in the text. It is much simpler to write "as Exhibit 4 shows," than "as shown in the table titled 'A Summary of Comparable Improved Sales.'" To assist the reader, it is better to call all the graphics "exhibits" and number them consecutively throughout the report. Some writers distinguish between tables and figures, identifying columns of numbers as tables and other graphics as figures. Although this is technically correct, assigning one numbering sequence to the tables and another to the figures can be very confusing. It is not uncommon, for example, to find Table 6 following Figure 9. To avoid this confusion, simply call everything an exhibit and a single numbering sequence will suffice.

Developing a Persuasive Reporting Style

An appraisal report is a persuasive document that sets forth sufficient evidence and provides adequate analysis to support the final estimate of value. Obviously the credibility of the conclusion depends primarily on the data and the analysis, but the way the appraiser's argument is presented to the client makes all the difference. Insightful, perceptive analysis has very little value unless it is presented to the client clearly and persuasively.

Many communication issues must be addressed to ensure that the language of an appraisal report does not obscure or detract from the clarity of the argument. The following suggestions highlight some of the most important components of good report writing.

AVOID A BLOATED WRITING STYLE.

Writing to express, not impress, is particularly important for appraisers because technical language, complicated procedures, and the sheer length of many reports create quite enough hurdles for the lay reader. Unfortunately, many people think that the way to succeed in writing is to use an impressive vocabulary and be long-winded—to pump it up. Some may have gotten this mistaken notion in school but, in the business world, such writing is doomed to failure.

In ordinary speech one might say simply, "The steady increase in rents and office property values and the community's strong economic base indicate that values should continue to rise in the near future." In writing a report, the same person may feel the need to pump it up, adding unnecessary verbiage:

> The appraiser is of the opinion after a careful examination of all the relevant data pertaining to the comparable and competitive market, including but not limited to the sale of office properties and the rents attained thereunto, as well as of the

strong fiscal data pertinent to the economic base for this community, that a continued rise in office type property values in the foreseeable future is considered to have a high probability, though, like all projections concerning the economy, this is not certain.

While this passage is an obvious exaggeration, the difficulty with such bloated writing is that the reader loses the main thought in a torrent of words. Unfortunately, some people believe that stilted language is evidence of true professionalism and that hedging your opinions is a requirement of the appraisal profession. Nothing could be further from the truth.

Today most business people live in a sea of words, which constantly threatens to overwhelm their reading time and their patience. What the writer wants to say must always be tempered by what the reader is willing to plow through.

DO NOT TRY TO SOUND LIKE A LAWYER.

Even the legal profession is struggling to eradicate pompous legal expressions. Archaic language serves no purpose other than to complicate communication. In the first half of this century, much business writing sounded like legal writing, but today such language is inappropriate. The following examples of legalese are pompous and usually unnecessary.

- pursuant
- heretofore
- appraisement
- herein
- finalize

- predicated
- consummate
- above-referenced
- fully cognizant
- opine

LET THE LITTLE WORDS DO THE WORK.

Good writing is full of one-syllable words. Don't use a large word when a small one will do. To eliminate "do-nothing" verbiage, change clauses to phrases and phrases to words. Replacing trite phrases with a single word results in a much denser, cleaner writing style. The following fat, flabby phrases say no more than their lean, muscular equivalents:

Instead of	Use
for the purpose of	to
with a view to	to
in order to	to
due to the fact that	because

Instead of	Use
in view of the fact	because
inasmuch as	because
for the reason that	because
with regard to	about
with reference to	about
with respect to	about
relative to	about
in the amount of	for
at a cost of	for
for a sum of	for
fully cognizant	aware
at this point in time	now
whether or not	whether
despite the fact that	although
at which time	when
a sufficient quantity of	enough
in the near future	soon
during the time that	while
by means of	by
in excess of	over/above
in view of the above	therefore
in the course of	during
the majority of	most
in conjunction with	with
in the event that	if
at the present time	now
a limited quantity of	few

The Appraisal Writing Handbook

The little word is always the better first choice; the longer phrases are not incorrect and may be used occasionally for variety or emphasis.

THOUGHTLESS REDUNDANCIES REFLECT CARELESS THINKING.

Redundancies often infiltrate writing simply because they are common in ordinary speech. Nevertheless, verbal carelessness has no place in thoughtful prose. Avoid the following:

my personal opinion	rectangular in shape
two equal halves	large in size
new innovation	consensus of opinion
past history	hot water heater

Occasionally a redundant phrase may be used for emphasis—*absolutely essential, exact replica,* or *just the same.* One common phrase, *close proximity,* is technically not a redundancy, but it should be used only to distinguish degrees of proximity. A more specific phrase (two blocks away, one-quarter mile away) is always more meaningful.

THE PHRASE "THE _____ OF" USUALLY CONTAINS DEADWOOD.

The unnecessary phrase *the _____ of* so often contains meaningless or obvious information that writers should become sensitive to its use. Notice the deadwood in the sentence, "The property sold for the amount of $930,000." No one needs to be told that $930,000 is an amount. The following list illustrates variants of this phrase that often contain useless filler:

...in the state of Maine....

...estimated at a cost of $2,900....

...during the month of April....

...rose to a level of 12.5%....

... located in the city of Detroit.

...are currently in the process of requesting....

Eliminating these empty phrases will help readers concentrate on what is important.

USE BEGINNINGS FOR SOMETHING IMPORTANT.

The beginning of a sentence, a paragraph, or even a whole section of the report should offer the reader something of significance. The reader is alert for new information early on, so it is inefficient to waste this valuable, attention-grabbing spot.

Sentences beginning with *there is, there are,* or *it is* squander the opening position with words that mean nothing. These formulaic phrases are meaningless and the sentence can be rewritten for greater emphasis. "There are five units currently vacant at the subject." can be recast as "Five units at the subject are currently vacant."

Paragraphs should begin with a topic sentence that expresses an attitude or opinion. Revealing an opinion at the beginning sparks the reader's interest in the discussion that follows. The remainder of the paragraph builds a case to support the opinion given in the topic sentence, and the idea is usually repeated more strongly in a concluding sentence. Avoid burying important ideas or conclusions in the middle of a paragraph.

Similarly, each major section of the report should begin with an attention-grabbing statement. Too often region and city descriptions begin with a limp, obvious sentence like, "The subject property is located in the city of Battle Creek, which is in the south-central part of the state of Michigan." This information is obviously important, but it is just a fact, not an enticing insight to engage the client's interest. If a major purpose of the region and city section is to reveal how this locale affects the values of properties like the subject, then it would be much more valuable to reveal right at the beginning the appraiser's general conclusion about the region and city. "Battle Creek, where the subject is located, has rebounded from the economic malaise that affected so many cities in southern Michigan during the early 1980s" is a much more useful opening for this section of the report. The revised sentence provides more information about the location and reveals a general trend to be analyzed in the discussion that follows.

BE PRECISE AND SPECIFIC.

Appraisal reports are filled with terms that require clarification. What, for example, does *stabilized occupancy* or *stabilized income* really mean? These terms can have various meanings, even among professionals. Without a specific explanation, the client is left to fall back on some vague notion that may not match the writer's intention. Be careful to avoid common, but vague, terminology.

Another area of potential confusion involves value-judgment phrases such as *a large tract* and *a superior location*. These phrases imply that the writer was impressed with the size or location, but the actual size of the tract and the reasons that the location is superior remain a mystery. These vague value judgments must be supported with facts to achieve effective communication.

BEWARE OF THE DANGERS OF BOILERPLATE.

The need for standardized language, or boilerplate, is obvious. Creating new introductions, background information, and explanations for every report is a waste of time and energy. Nevertheless, the use of boilerplate is dangerous. First, standardized sections are usually designed to fit into every conceivable assignment, so they frequently present explanations of procedures and theoretical discussions that are beyond the scope of the given appraisal assignment. For example, a standard introduction to the income capitalization approach may describe several methods of estimating a capitalization rate when only a single method is used in the appraisal. Explaining procedures and techniques that don't apply to the specific appraisal in question simply pads the report and overwhelm the client with irrelevant information. The best solution is to design boilerplate that can be easily tailored to suit the specific appraisal assignment or to keep the standard sections used very brief and general.

Attempting to use a standard region and city description for every appraisal of a property in a particular city is extremely dangerous. Not only do the facts and data quickly become outdated, but every property type requires a slightly different perspective because different regional and city characteristics will be more or less significant. Major trucking routes, for example, are important in appraisals of industrial warehouses but are less important in the valuation of multifamily housing. Conversely, the proximity of schools and places of worship may affect the values of residential properties, but typically will have little impact on commercial properties. A boilerplate description of the region and city designed to cover every property type will be unnecessarily long and include much information that is irrelevant to the assignment at hand. In fact, most appraisers find that these standardized sections get longer and longer over the years.

An alternative to presenting long, standardized region and city descriptions is to break up the descriptions into many, small subtopics. In this way the writer can use only those sections that have specific relevance to the assignment and edit each to suit the property being appraised. Tailoring these standardized sections to the property type is an easy way to make this important part of the report appear more integral to the analysis. The region and city description lays the groundwork for much of the material that appears later in the report, so it is crucial that it not be buried in boilerplate. Making this section shorter and more property-specific increases the chances that clients will actually read it.

JARGON CREATES A HURDLE FOR THE NONPROFESSIONAL READER.

Every profession has specialized terminology and language that expedites communication among the cognoscenti in the field. These terms have very precise meanings known to the initiated, but lay clients may find them bewildering. Remember that many nonappraisers react to appraisal jargon just as appraisers react to a doctor's Latin medical terms.

Be sensitive to the problems that jargon can create and provide clear explanations with good, concrete examples for lay readers. The alternative is to quote professional definitions, but these are often too complex for an outsider. For example, *The Dictionary of Real Estate Appraisal,* third edition, defines a short-lived item as "a building component with an expected remaining economic life that is shorter than the remaining economic life of the entire structure," which is perfectly accurate. However, the only type of reader who needs a definition, the poor lay reader, is left to puzzle over the *economic life* of building components. If the appraiser instead writes that "short-lived items in a building are those items that need periodic replacement during the life of a typical building, such as carpeting, paint, and water heaters," the nonappraiser has the explanation he or she needs to follow the analysis. The goal of an appraisal report is to communicate clearly, so be sure the words used are intelligible to the average reader.

DO NOT STEW THE READER IN ALPHABET SOUP.

Everyone has at some time picked up a government journal or a professional article from an unfamiliar field and been confronted with a conundrum of mysterious acronyms. Imagine the nonappraiser's frustration with sentences or tables full of *IRR, PV, PGIM,* MUD, *GBA, GLA,* ACMs, ACRS, and *NPV.* Even more frustrating are unexplained symbols, like R_O, R_L, Y_B, and Y_O. Although common among professional appraisers, these terms are not part of the everyday language of most clients. The accepted practice is to write out a term in full the first time it is used and to show the corresponding acronym or symbol in parentheses. In preparing tables, be sure to provide a key to symbols and unfamiliar abbreviations. Be considerate of readers and try to limit the number of acronyms and symbols used.

AVOID THE TRITE AND OVERUSED.

Many business writers fall back on buzz words and hackneyed phrases. Widespread usage does not excuse their triteness, vagueness, and, in some cases, grammatical incorrectness. Instead of succumbing to the trite, strive for language that is simple and precise. The following words and phrases should be avoided or used with great care:

utilize	very unique	at this point in time
finalize	input	predicated on the assumption
normalize	in receipt of	impact (as a verb)
prioritize	our records show	bottom line
in lieu of	remittance	opine
stabilized	the utmost care	sincerely hope

VERBS ASSERT THE MEANING.

Our language is constantly changing, often to accommodate technological change. For example, the noun *fax* (from facsimile) is now acceptably used as a verb, *to fax*. However, it is best for report writers not to be in the vanguard of these changes. Marketing people often use attention-grabbing devices in writing, such as the currently popular practice of "verbing," turning standard verbs into new and unusual verbs. Do not be the first to jump on the bandwagon with "He merely ballparked the number." or "They back-burnered the project." Odd usage has no place in formal appraisal reports.

On the other hand, verbs give a sentence punch. Good writing is full of strong, active verbs; without them writing can be lackluster and limp. Consequently, writers should avoid using nouns when an equivalent, assertive verb is at hand.

Use	emphasize	*not*	place emphasis on
	suggest	*not*	is our suggestion
	need	*not*	be in need of
	reduce	*not*	effect a reduction in
	conclude	*not*	bring to a conclusion
	think	*not*	it is our opinion that
	use	*not*	make use of or utilization
	must	*not*	is required to
	indicate	*not*	is an indication that

WRITE IN THE ACTIVE VOICE.

Almost everyone has been admonished to write in the active, not the passive, voice. Virtually every grammar and style-checking software package highlights passive voice sentences and suggests revising them. Anyone who has run one of these software programs on a typical appraisal report knows the prevalence of the passive voice in appraisal writing. The passive voice is often considered boring, but that is not the most pressing reason to avoid its use in appraisal reports. Before discussing other reasons, consider the difference between passive and active voice sentences.

In active voice sentences, the subject performs the action :

> **Subject + active verb + object**
>
> I inspected the property.
>
> James Thomas interviewed the owners.
>
> Buyers can usually obtain financing.
>
> The zoning commission will change the requirements.

In each of these sentences, the subject performs the action expressed by the verb. In passive voice sentences, the subject does not perform the action and the verb changes to the passive voice by the addition of some form of the helping, or auxiliary, verb *to be*.

> **Subject + passive verb + prepositional phrase with "by"**
>
> The property was inspected by me.
>
> The owners were interviewed by James Thomas.
>
> Financing usually can be obtained by buyers.
>
> The requirements will be changed by the zoning commission.

Notice that the subject of the active sentence becomes the object of a prepositional phrase beginning with *by* in the passive version, and the active sentence's object becomes the subject of the passive sentence.

The passive voice is a perfectly acceptable grammatical form and it is even preferable in a few instances, that is, when assigning blame or when the individual or agent who performed the action is unknown or insignificant.

> The report was finished late. (The guilty party is not stated out of politeness.)
>
> The property was poorly maintained, resulting in extensive water damage. (The individual responsible is not known.)

Extensive use of the passive voice, however, produces ponderously dull prose, for all the action is drained out of the sentence. The subject, what or who we are talking about, never does anything.

A more significant reason to avoid overuse of the passive voice is that the passive voice changes the whole focus of the report. It becomes a report about the appraiser instead of one about the market and the data. The following passage is fairly typical of much appraisal writing:

> An adjustment for superior location was derived (by me) by comparing Sales 2 and 4, which were considered (by me) similar except for location. Based on this pairing, a 10% adjustment was applied (by me) to compensate for superior location.

Obviously the phrases in parentheses do not appear in the report, but the reader clearly hears them. This continual, subtle allusion to the appraiser shifts the focus from the facts and the market to the appraiser. The 10% adjustment mentioned arises from the market data, not simply from the appraiser's mind.

Rewriting the passage in the active voice, without reference to the writer, places the emphasis where it belongs.

> A comparison of Sales 2 and 4, which are similar except for location, indicates a 10% adjustment to compensate for superior location.

In this revision the appraiser does not appear. The adjustment arises from the market data, not from the appraiser's action or opinion—a much more accurate and persuasive description of the adjustment process.

CHAPTER 4

Selling the Value Conclusion

Appraisers must be objective when performing the valuation analysis, but when the analysis is done and the value conclusion has been reached, the situation changes. In the reporting process, the writer must be an advocate for the conclusions in the report. A good report presents the information and analysis in a manner that a reader will both understand and believe. An appraisal report is a persuasive argument presented to support a reasonable conclusion. The following sections describe many techniques that can increase the effectiveness of the appraiser's persuasive argument.

FOCUS ON THE MARKET AND THE FACTS.

The subject of any appraisal is the market, yet so many appraisal reports inadvertently focus on the appraiser instead. As discussed in Chapter 3, overuse of the passive voice is the most frequent cause of "appraiser focus." Although the passive voice has its uses, writing in the active voice, without reference to the author of the report, allows the facts to speak for themselves.

Another, less frequent, problem is the misconception that an appraisal report is primarily a record of what the appraiser did. To some extent a report does need to record that the analyst has performed certain actions: the properties were inspected, the sales data was confirmed, and the data was verified. These facts clearly need to be recorded, but once a writer begins to report his or her actions, it is easy to fall into the trap of memoir writing. After describing the specific actions performed, the appraiser can present the analysis based on what the facts and procedures show, rather than providing a record of what the writer did, found, and concluded about the facts.

USE *I* AND *WE* JUDICIOUSLY.

Although high school English teachers may insist that first person pronouns have no place in formal writing, what they really mean is that formal writing should not focus on the writer. Nevertheless, appraisal reports often need to refer to things the appraiser has done, such as inspections, interviews, or research, and making these statements in the first person is perfectly acceptable. In fact, *I* is preferable to the very awkward and pompous *the appraiser.* If the client needs to know who inspected a property or interviewed an individual, then reveal that information with *I, we,* or the individual's name, rather than use the stilted third person. Nevertheless, a typical report should require very few references to the writer and, consequently, very few uses of *I* or *we.*

AVOID UNNECESSARY HEDGING.

"An appraisal is full of many things I can never know for sure, but there is one thing I always know with absolute certainty: my opinion!"

Ultimately, an appraisal is an opinion. That opinion is not plucked out of thin air, rather it is the result of market research and the application of well-established appraisal theory and procedures. The final estimate of value in a report is an opinion, but only insofar as any conclusion arising from an analysis is ultimately an opinion.

Many appraisers feel a need to remind the client constantly that virtually all conclusions formed during the analysis are opinions, perhaps to ensure that these opinions do not masquerade as facts. No knowledgeable reader will be misled by conclusions stated assertively if the market data and logic leading to the conclusions have been fully revealed. The following statement needs no qualification or hedge words:

> Because it is at the intersection of two heavily traveled streets and has excellent accessibility, Sale 2's location is superior to the subject's.

To weaken this conclusion with *it is considered to have, it is thought to have, it is the appraiser's opinion that,* or any other hedge phrases is unnecessary. After all, the sale's superiority results from facts, not from opinion, and omitting the qualifiers cannot be construed as misleading, even by the most tenacious attorney.

There is no legal justification to hedge every conclusion in a report, and these hedge phrases detract immensely from the report's persuasiveness. If every conclusion in the analysis has been stated so that it sounds like mere opinion, it should come as no surprise to find that the client is not convinced by the final value conclusion. Of course, hedging is sometimes necessary. Appraisers are frequently asked to forecast economic trends, interpret market activity and cycles, and use client-provided financial reports as a basis for estimating value. In such instances, truth demands that the writer hedge his or her conclusions with words such as *is reported to be, seems, appears, should,* and *approximately.* Any broad generalization requires some kind of qualifying word or phrase to leave room for unforeseen exceptions to the rule. Like the passive voice, hedging has a valid place in appraisal reports, but should not be overused.

Unfortunately, hedging can be addictive. Qualifying words and phrases creep into sentences where they serve no legitimate purpose. Stop and think before using these common hedge words and phrases:

is considered	is thought to be	is felt somewhat
in my opinion	appears	is reported to be
is believed	is deemed	appraiser's opinion
more or less	among others	

The use of careful qualifications where needed and forceful, hedge-free statements of most professional judgments can produce a report that is both accurate and persuasive. Do not let excessive hedging weaken an otherwise strong report.

THE PRESENT TENSE USUALLY STRENGTHENS THE ARGUMENT.

The present tense gives an immediacy to a piece of writing. Unfortunately, many appraisal reports are couched in the past tense: sales "were adjusted," "were utilized," or "were superior or inferior." Such writing again focuses on the appraiser and sounds like a memoir. For the most part, an appraisal report is not simply a history of what the appraiser did, but a position statement of what the appraiser thinks and what the facts reveal.

Compare the following sample passages, the first written in the past tense and the second in the present tense:

> A band of investment was performed, and it indicated an overall capitalization rate of 10.5. The mortgage component was calculated using current financing available. The equity component was derived based on the financing terms involved in three sales discussed in the Sales Comparison Approach. These three sales indicated a tight range of equity capitalization rates, which supported the chosen equity rate, which was the only real variable in the analysis.

> The following band of investment indicates an overall capitalization rate of 10.5. Current available financing terms provide the basis for the mortgage component. The equity component is based on the financing terms involved in three sales discussed in the Sales Comparison Approach. The equity capitalization rates from these three sales form a tight range, which supports the equity rate selected—the only real variable in the analysis.

The first sample stresses what the appraiser did and is a history of actions performed. The second sample, on the other hand, concentrates on the analysis and the data; it is a statement of what the analysis shows. In a subtle way, the present tense lends greater credibility to the report. It says, "This is what the facts show and what I think." rather than "This was what I did and what I thought."

Appraisal reports cannot be written entirely in the present tense, for often appraisers must report what they or others did or said. These statements must remain in the past tense, but the bulk of the analysis and all of the conclusions can be presented much more persuasively in the present tense.

REVEAL THE ANALYSIS WHEN RECONCILING WITHIN A RANGE.

Reconciling within a range is typically not a mathematical process. Instead, it involves "fuzzy" logic and judgment. The need to make many reasoned judgments in an appraisal goes a long way toward justifying the very existence of the appraisal profession. It is in the reconciliation process that experience, knowledge, and professional analysis reveal themselves. Reconciling within ranges is what appraisers do.

All three approaches to value involve reconciling the range of market data found. The sales comparison approach is essentially one huge reconciliation of the unadjusted sale prices of comparable properties. Analytical techniques such as paired data analysis, regression analysis, and the adjustment process help to quantify this reconciliation, but throughout the analysis the appraiser must make numerous judgments about the ranges in the data. Each of these small reconciliations is an opinion that could be contested, and the credibility of the final value estimate depends on the validity of the numerous reconciliations that precede it.

Each reconciliation in a report should present a logical argument in miniature. Each conclusion involves thoughtful reasoning and analysis. No professional appraiser simply picks a number at random, and no report should make these conclusions sound arbitrary. The writer must reveal the logical thought process leading to the conclusion. How much discussion each conclusion requires will depend, in part, on how significant it is within the particular approach to value. For example, reconciling the range of insurance cost estimates typically affects the net operating income very little, so little discussion is necessary. Conversely, reconciling among the various capitalization rates derived from the market has an immense impact on the value indication, even when the range is tight. The discussion supporting this crucial reconciliation should be much more analytical and persuasive. The task is not to analyze more, but simply to describe more of the analysis within the report.

RECONCILE WITHIN RANGES METHODICALLY.

The primary goal of a well-written reconciliation is to provide a logical argument leading to an inevitable conclusion. The reader should be able to predict the conclusion from the preceding discussion.

Sometimes the reconciliation is relatively simple. For example, the market may provide only two indicators, and one is clearly better. At other times, the indicators are more numerous and complex, so the discussion is more difficult to communicate. Complicated analyses may be required to reconcile the ranges of adjusted sale prices for land and improved property sales, market rent indicators, and market-derived capitalization rates. Each of these sections of the report will call for careful thought and persuasive writing.

The following devices will help writers create reader-friendly reconciliations:

- Know the conclusion before beginning to write.

- Recognize that the writer is much more familiar with the data than readers are. The readers have seen the adjustment grid in the sales comparison approach, but they cannot be expected to remember that Sale 4's adjusted price is $115.65 per square foot while Sale 2's price is only $98.50 per square foot.

- Consider arraying the adjusted sales data from high to low, even if an adjustment grid appears on an earlier page. Adjustment grids are typically arrayed by sale number, but the sale numbers do not correspond to the adjusted sale prices.

- Organize the discussion logically. If one indicator deserves no weight, eliminate it first. If the final conclusion is at the top of the range, work from the lowest to the highest comparable; do the opposite if the conclusion is at the bottom of the range. Arriving at a conclusion in the middle of the range usually involves dispensing with the extremes and working toward the middle.

- Avoid a mathematically derived conclusion. Averages or weighted averages seldom persuade readers.

- Use the reconciliation to discuss the factors influencing sale prices that could not be adjusted for quantitatively. Instead of making an unsupported adjustment for a certain characteristic, discuss the influence of that factor in the reconciliation and explain what that indicates about the probable sale price of the subject. For example, the appraiser might write,

> Sale 3 is the only comparable in inferior condition. Although no data exists to support a specific adjustment, its inferior condition helps to explain why Sale 3 is at the bottom of the range, and the subject should sell for a significantly higher price.

THE FINAL RECONCILIATION OF VALUE MERITS A THOROUGH DISCUSSION AND A PERSUASIVE ARGUMENT.

The final reconciliation of value is the last element in the report and, consequently, it often receives less attention than it deserves. The final reconciliation is critical. It is the appraiser's opportunity to speak directly to the client about the relative strengths and weaknesses of the supporting data, the numerous judgments made, and the various procedures used in the three approaches. In the discussion of each approach, the appraiser's goal has been simply to arrive at a value indication. At the end of the report, the appraiser can step back from the whole process and assess the relative validity of each value indication.

Occasionally writers misinterpret the directive to discuss the strengths and weaknesses of the approaches by focusing on their theoretical strengths and weaknesses, rather than their applicability to the subject property. Theoretically, all three approaches are equally valid. What strengthens or weakens an approach is the quality and quantity of the market data available for analysis. For example, one frequently hears that the cost approach is weakened by the need to estimate depreciation. This may be true, but it is not a theoretical weakness. It usually results from the lack of good market data to support the estimate.

An effective final reconciliation should:

- Establish the problem (the different value indications) and proceed methodically to reach a conclusion.

- Avoid merely summarizing the application of each approach. Listing the analyses performed does not address the real problem—determining which approach provides the best indicator.

- Discuss the quantity and comparability of the data available for analysis: Were there enough similar sales? Was the market data reliable and recent? Did the market data fall into a narrow or wide range?

- Reveal the appraiser's level of confidence concerning the significant judgments made in each approach. Was there good market data to support the adjustments in the sales comparison approach? Were the ranges tight enough to indicate clear choices?

- Avoid bias for or against each approach to value and avoid sweeping generalities about the three approaches.

- Address the real question regarding each approach: Relative to the other two approaches, how good is the value indication derived from this approach?

- Lead the reader methodically to the conclusion. This usually means that the discussion of the best approach is presented last and never buried as the second of three approaches discussed.

- Provide enough persuasive discussion so that the reader can predict the final estimate of value or, at least, not be surprised by it.

CHAPTER 5

Achieving Correctness in Appraisal Reports

Even an excellent appraisal analysis is diminished if it is communicated in a report that has typos, grammatical errors, and usage problems. The carelessness in the writing inevitably reflects on the quality of the appraiser's argument. Editing a report for correctness is one of the last steps in the reporting process and it is very important. No one should eliminate this crucial task to meet a deadline.

Don't be too concerned about proper grammar, usage, and punctuation in writing the first draft. For some people this can cause writer's block. When drafting a report, it is best to focus on getting your thoughts on paper. Polishing, perfecting, and correcting will come later, in the editing process.

The following sections address topics of concern to appraisers and of importance in writing appraisal reports. Many exhaustive studies of grammar, punctuation, and usage are available, but few address the problems unique to the appraisal profession.

PRESENT NUMBERS CORRECTLY AND EFFECTIVELY.

Numbers are the basis for appraisal reports. To help the reader comprehend the barrage of numbers presented, however, the writer must remember a few basic principles. First, prose and numerals do not mix well. Most readers find it difficult to remember more than a few numbers in a single paragraph. If it is necessary to present several numbers in the narrative, keep the paragraph short. It is preferable to present numbers in a table or calculation set off with white space. Second, avoid mysterious numbers. Always provide a label and source of derivation to put the information in context for the reader.

Appraisal reports generally fall into the category of technical writing, which means that certain rules about presenting numbers should be applied. These guidelines may differ from those most people were taught in English class. Following these rules should ensure that numbers are presented clearly in appraisal reports.

Rule 1. Write out all numbers less than 10.
The numbers one through nine are normally written out.

three comparable sales

two recent transactions

seven years

An exception to this rule concerns numbers used with standard units of measure (such as square feet, hours, percentages, dollars), page numbers, and dates.

9 miles	9 a.m.	8%
2-month delay	page 6	during the early 1990s
$2.50	2 sq. ft.	

Any number greater than nine is usually expressed in numerals.

16 sales	254 acres	10 properties

Rule 2. Place a hyphen between the number and the unit of measure when they modify a noun.

two-bedroom
apartment   5-year lease   220-volt circuit

Note that *bedroom* is not a standard unit of measure, whereas *year* is. This explains why one number is written out and the other is not.

Rule 3. Write decimals and fractions as numerals.
0.167   ½

Whenever possible, write fractions as decimals.

0.375   *not 3/8*

Always place a zero before the decimal in numbers less than one.

0.12   *not .12*
$0.45   *not $.45*

Rule 4. Do not imply an unwarranted level of accuracy.
Use of a decimal implies precision to the last decimal place. To write "0.50 mile" suggests accuracy to a hundredth of a mile. To report this distance as an approximation, as is common in appraisal reports, write "one-half mile." To speak of one-quarter, one-half, or three-quarters of a mile implies an approximation, so it is redundant to add words such as

approximately, roughly, about, or *more or less.* Beware of absurdities like
"approximately 263.078± acres."

Rule 5. When many numbers appear in the same paragraph, write them all as numerals.
Numerals are much easier to grasp than words. Shifting from words for
numbers under 10 to numerals for others is inconsistent and confusing.
Stick with numerals in passages that contain many numbers.

Rule 6. Never begin a sentence with a numeral.
The first word of a sentence can be a number, but it must be written out
as a word. Usually it is preferable to rearrange the order of the sentence,
for long numbers written as words can be grotesque.

Use	Two hundred acres remain undeveloped.
not	200 acres remain undeveloped.
Use	The property has 272 undeveloped acres.
not	Two hundred seventy-two acres remain undeveloped.

Rule 7. Presenting numbers in both numerals and words is usually not appropriate.
Lawyers commonly express numbers in both words and numerals—thirty
(30) days—so that no unscrupulous person can alter the document. To
follow this practice throughout an appraisal report is to suggest something
unpleasant about the client, and it unnecessarily complicates the writing.
In two instances, however, numbers should be written in the legal style
using both words and numerals: the estimates of value in the letter of
transmittal and in the final reconciliation section of the appraisal report.

$250,000 (two hundred fifty thousand dollars)

SUBJECTS AND VERBS MUST AGREE IN NUMBER.
Singular subjects need singular verbs and plural subjects need plural verbs:
"The property is..." and "The properties are...." Errors in subject-verb
agreement are the most common grammatical problem in appraisal
reports, probably because of the length and complexity of the sentences.
Some guidelines follow:

- The subject never appears in a prepositional phrase. Do not be
  confused by prepositional phrases between the subject and the verb.
  In the following sentence, the subject is *each*, not *properties*, which is
  the object of a prepositional phrase.

  Each of the five properties sold recently in both of
  these areas *was....*

- Two or more subjects joined by *and* always take a plural verb.

    Sale 1 and Sale 4 *were* eliminated from the analysis

- Two or more subjects joined by *or, nor, neither...nor,* or *either...or* take verbs that agree with the nearer subject.

    Neither the subject nor the comparable properties *were*....

    Neither the comparable properties nor the subject *was*....

- *There* is never the subject of a sentence. In sentences beginning with *there*, the verb must agree with the real subject, which in these constructions always comes after the verb.

    There are several new projects coming on line.

    Projects is the subject of the sentence.

- A singular subject followed by *in addition to, as well as, including,* or *no less than* requires a singular verb. What follows these phrases is not part of the subject and does not influence the subject-verb agreement. Often these sentences sound awkward because grammar dictates that a singular verb be used although the subject is logically plural. These sentences can generally be rewritten so that the logic and the grammar agree.

    The subject as well as the three comparable sales *is*.... (grammatically correct)

    The subject and the three comparable sales *are*.... (both logical and grammatical)

- Many indefinite pronouns take singular verbs, even those that convey plural concepts. Don't be fooled by pronouns ending with *body, thing,* or *one*. The following pronouns are always singular:

this	anyone	anybody	anything
another	everyone	everybody	everything
each	no one	nobody	nothing
either	someone	somebody	something
neither	one		

AVOID UNGRAMMATICAL AND SEXIST PRONOUN REFERENCES.

A pronoun refers to (or renames) a noun or another pronoun, and it must agree with that noun or pronoun in both number and gender. For example, refer to *Tom* with the singular masculine pronoun *he* or *him* and to *Mary* with *she* or *her*. Gender is important only with singular references because *they* and *them* are gender neutral.

Problems occur because English has no neutral singular pronoun. Traditionally, the masculine pronoun is used: "An appraiser should proofread *his* report" or "Everyone should proofread *his* report." In the past two decades, new social awareness and changes in the workplace have made use of the masculine pronoun unacceptable to many people. Attempts to avoid the sexist implications of this usage have produced awkward revisions such as:

> Each appraiser should proofread their report. (Ungrammatical because *each appraiser* requires a singular pronoun reference.)

> An appraiser should proofread *his* or *her* report. (Acceptable, but cumbersome if used repeatedly.)

A preferable means of revision is to use a plural subject and replace *his* or *her* with *their*. Alternatively, the writer can totally rewrite the sentence to avoid any gender reference.

> All appraisers should proofread their reports carefully.

> An appraiser should proofread a report carefully.

> An appraiser should proofread carefully.

USE *WHO, THAT,* AND *WHICH* CORRECTLY.

Who refers only to people (as do its other forms *whom, whose, whomever, whoever, whosoever,* and *whomsoever*). *That* refers both to people and things (including animals). *Which* refers only to things and animals (never to people).

Normally, *that* introduces clauses necessary to the sentence's meaning (restrictive) and *which* introduces unnecessary (nonrestrictive) clauses. Clauses beginning with *which*, like other elements that interrupt a sentence, are set off with commas.

> The property *that* sold most recently is three miles from the subject.

> Sale 2, *which* sold most recently, is three miles from the subject.

The clause in the first sample is necessary because it identifies the particular property; the clause in the second sentence merely provides additional information about Sale 2.

USE THE RIGHT WORD.

The following words are frequently misused.

affect, effect

Affect is always a verb meaning to act upon or to influence.

> Motivation can *affect* the sale price.

Effect usually is a noun meaning the result or consequence.

> Measuring the *effect* of motivation on the sale price is difficult.

Effect can occasionally act as a verb meaning to bring about or to cause to happen. This usage always involves an agent or catalyst—the speaker (or subject) can only influence or prompt, not do it alone.

> The owners will try to *effect* a zoning variance.

aggravate

Aggravate is used colloquially to mean to irritate or annoy. In standard, formal English, it means to make worse or intensify.

> The opening of a new regional mall has *aggravated* the vacancy problems of retail properties in the neighborhood.

allude, refer

Allude means to touch on lightly or mention indirectly; *refer* means to mention distinctly and directly.

amount, number

Amount applies to a mass or bulk, while *number* is used for separate units.

> A large *number* of properties had a great *amount* of land.

as, like

As introduces a clause and *like* introduces a phrase.

> ...they acted *as* cautious buyers should.

> ...they acted *like* cautious buyers.

capital, capitol

Capital refers to a seat of government or money invested, or it may mean foremost. *Capitol* refers only to a government building.

comparable

Comparable is really an adjective, as in "a comparable property," but in speech real estate professionals frequently use *comparable* as a noun, as in "the only recent comparable is..." This noun form is less acceptable in formal writing. Note also that the correct pronunciation of the word has the accent on the first syllable (COMParable, not comPARable).

complement, compliment

Complement or *complementary* refers to that which completes or goes well with.

> The addition differs from, but *complements,* the original structure.

Compliment and *complimentary* refer to flattery or praise.

> The clients were very *complimentary* about the report.

continual, continuous

Continual implies a regular, but interrupted, succession. *Continuous* suggests a constant, uninterrupted succession.

> The *continual* rains affected the tourist business.

> The *continuous* demand for housing increased property values.

credible, creditable

Credible refers to something that is believable.

> Their forecasts were *credible,* given the positive data available at the time.

Creditable refers to something that is praiseworthy.

> They did a *creditable* job, given the scarce data available. ·

data

Data is widely accepted today as a singular noun. Strictly speaking, *data* is the plural of *datum* and should be followed by a plural verb. Many academic publishers and scientific professionals still prefer "these data are...." On the other hand, most business writers now use "the data is...," and this is grammatically acceptable.

e.g., i.e.

From the Latin *exempli gratia, e.g.,* means "for example." From the Latin *id est, i.e.,* means "that is." So many readers confuse these two abbreviations that it is usually better to avoid the Latin and use "for example" and "that is" instead.

farther, further

Farther refers to distance.

> The property is five miles *farther* from the airport.

Further refers to degree or quantity.

> They decided to investigate the matter *further.*

fewer, less

Fewer applies to number and to things that are countable; it modifies plural nouns. *Less* applies to quantity, to things that are measured but not counted; it modifies singular nouns.

> *Fewer* buyers in the market suddenly caused *less* demand for single-family houses.

imply, infer

Imply means to suggest or hint. A writer or speaker *implies* something to the reader or listener. *Infer* means to conclude or derive from. The listener *infers* information from what is said.

> The buyer *implied* that she wanted advantageous seller financing, so the owners *inferred* that they could renegotiate the sale price.

is when, is where

Do not use *is when* or *is where* in definitions. Time and location are not at issue. Do not write, "An arm's-length transaction *is when* the buyer and seller ...."

principle, principal

Principle has only one meaning: a basic truth, rule, or assumption.

> The *principle* of substitution holds that....
>
> One *principle* to live by is....

Principal has many meanings. As an adjective it may mean primary or most important. As a noun, *principal* may refer to money invested, a major player (in an investment), or the director of a school.

> A *principal* in the deal gave his *principal* reason for losing his *principal* in the investment.

unique

Unique means the only one of its kind. It cannot be modified because there are no degrees of uniqueness. Similar words that can be modified or compared are *unusual, rare,* and *outstanding.* One can say "a very unusual property," but not "a very unique property."

within, in

For most descriptions of location, *in* is quite adequate.

> A property is *in* a neighborhood or city.

When speaking of boundaries, however, *within* is the correct word.

> The property is *within* the neighborhood boundaries...or *within* the city limits....

USE APOSTROPHES CORRECTLY.

The apostrophe is used to show possession. Sometimes the possessive expresses obvious ownership, as in "the company's property" or "Tom's report." In other cases the relationship is more subtle, for example:

> *In descriptions:* The building's foundation, the market's reaction
>
> *In measuring:* a year's income, a dollar's worth
>
> *To show purpose:* women's college (a school for women), men's locker room (a locker room for men)

Nouns need an apostrophe when they act as adjectives to modify a noun.

In speech the apostrophe has no function simply because it has no sound; it only matters in writing. An *s* at the end of a word does not always mean "more than one." Be alert to why the final *s* is there.

The rule about apostrophes that everyone remembers is: The apostrophe goes before the *s* if it's singular, and after the *s* when it's plural." For many words this rule is fine, but it simply does not work in all cases. Strunk and White's *The Elements of Style,* a classic reference work, advocates using *'s* for all singular nouns, but it leaves one to founder with plural nouns.

The easiest and most consistent process for using apostrophes is

1. Write the noun (singular or plural).

2. Add the apostrophe.

3. If there is no *s* at the end of the word already, add one.

This three-step procedure is technically correct in all instances. The only controversy concerns singular nouns ending in *s*, like *boss* or *Thomas*. The three-step procedure produces *boss'* and *Thomas'*, which are correct. Equally correct, however, are *boss's* and *Thomas's*. Some prefer to use the extra *s* here because people pronounce the extra *s* sound. Examples of singular and plural possessives follow:

property's	properties'	child's	children's
woman's	women's	house's	houses'
addendum's	addenda's	process's	processes'

The three-step rule also works for proper names like *Thomas,* which becomes *Thomas'* or *Thomas's* for the singular possessive and *Thomases'* for the plural possessive.

With compound nouns like *attorney general* and *bill of lading,* the writer makes the most significant word plural and then follows the three-step rule.

singular possessive	**plural possessive**
attorney general's	attorneys general's
bill of lading's	bills of lading's

Many plural possessives appear awkward. When the correct form is grotesque, consider using a prepositional phrase with *of* to express the possessive. For example, instead of *bills of lading's,* write *of the bills of lading.*

Personal pronouns show possession without using an apostrophe. Be sure not to use apostrophes with any of the following:

my, mine	our, ours
your, yours	their, theirs
her, hers	whose (*who's* means *who is*)

The Appraisal Writing Handbook

his	whomever
its (*it's* means *it is*)	whosoever

Using an apostrophe to make an acronym plural has fallen out of fashion. This particularly true when no periods are used in the acronym, as is most common today. The correct plurals for common appraisal acronyms follow:

NOIs	*GIMs*	*DCFs*	*IRRs*

Similarly, the plurals of dates can be expressed without the apostrophe (the 1980s), although using the apostrophe is also correct.

CHAPTER 6

Punctuation Guide

This brief guide to punctuation is not intended to be exhaustive. Rather, it covers the high points, answering the most frequently asked questions and ignoring basic rules that virtually everyone knows.

A very readable, comprehensive book on punctuation is Harry Shaw's *Punctuate It Right,* published by Harper & Row. A less thorough, more humorous guide is *The Well-Tempered Sentence* by Karen Elizabeth Gordon.

Punctuation is not a matter of personal style. It is based on rules designed to help readers understand narrative writing. While some controversy exists concerning unusual sentence structures, virtually all authorities agree on the principles set forth here. Grasping these major concepts will solve most punctuation problems. The most important goal is clarity. What punctuation provides the reader with the greatest clarity?

COMMAS

Commas are primarily used to separate parts of a sentence for clarity.

Commas set off expressions that interrupt the sentence.

* Appositives, words or phrases that rename or clarify a preceding word, are set off with commas.

> Frank, the president, and Diana, the sales manager, arrived yesterday.

> Her major task, finding new clients, takes most of her time.

Omit the commas if the appositive is closely associated with the noun it renames.

> my uncle Frank   the poet Keats   the explorer Columbus

- Direct address, calling the reader by name, is set off with commas.

  We would be happy, Mr. Wakefield, to send you additional information.

  You, Tom, are the first one to complete the project.

- Interrupting words and parenthetical expressions are set off with commas. Some common examples are *consequently, for example, on the other hand, yes, namely,* and the expressions set off with commas in the following sentences.

  Many expressions, however, are not necessary to the basic meaning of the sentence. In fact, most words or phrases that can be left out are parenthetical.

- Nonrestrictive clauses are set off with commas. Nonrestrictive clauses, which are incomplete sentences within the main sentence, usually begin with *who, which, whose,* or *whom.* They merely add information and could be omitted without changing the basic meaning of the sentence.

  The Roxy Theater, which was built in 1938, has a heating system that does not conform to code.

  John Cody, who works at Xerox, asked for a brochure that describes the maintenance procedures on the XL47.

- Clauses that are necessary to the meaning of a sentence should not be set off with commas. In some cases, adding commas would radically change the meaning.

  Our staff appraisers who significantly increased production will receive bonuses. (Only a few get bonuses.)

  Our staff appraisers, who significantly increased production, will receive bonuses. (Everyone gets a bonus.)

- Other word groups that interrupt to give nonessential information are also set off with commas. The most common interrupters are participial phrases and infinitive phrases. Some are restrictive, telling which one, and these require no commas; others are nonrestrictive, giving additional information, and commas are needed.

  Trees for Dry Places, listing the information you requested, is enclosed.

  A brochure listing the information you requested is enclosed.

  Diane Johnson, to give you an example, recently received her SRA designation.

Commas set off word groups that introduce.

- At the beginning of a sentence, use commas after adverbial clauses, which often begin with words such as *because, if, when, before, whenever, after,* and *although.*

  Before we deliver a report, three people proofread it.

  Although everyone was satisfied, we still hope to improve the procedure.

- If the adverbial clause appears in the middle or at the end of the sentence, use commas only if the clause is unnecessary to the meaning.

  He went to Cleveland before the news arrived.

  He went to Cleveland Tuesday, before the news arrived.

- Use commas after introductory modifying phrases if they are long or if they are widely separated from the word they modify. Short phrases, like a single prepositional phrase, usually do not need a separating comma.

  Discovering that two of the adjustment grids were missing, we notified your office immediately.

  By following the advice of his brother-in-law, Chris lost $500 in one hour at Las Vegas.

Commas separate parts of a sentence.

- Commas separate words or groups of words in a series.

  The appraisal includes the cost, sales comparison, and income capitalization approaches.

  Development of the new highway interchange, the city's rezoning of the area, and the sudden demand for vacant land have caused a dramatic increase in land values.

  Some people omit the comma between the last two items in a series joined by *and* or *or,* but this can sometimes cause confusion.

- If two or more adjectives equally modify the same noun, separate them with a comma. To know if they are equal, try to rearrange them. If doing so distorts the meaning, they are not equal and should not be separated with a comma.

a huge, old tree	a huge, old maple tree
shorter, clearer reports	shorter, clearer appraisal reports
an old, abandoned town	an old ghost town

- Commas separate main clauses (independent sentences) joined by *and, or, nor, but, for,* or *yet.*

Susan Jones took over our Denver office, yet no one has been found to replace her for the Boulder operation.

All of those reports were completed last Thursday, and we will start the next batch within two weeks.

- Commas separate the parts of dates and addresses.

On July 10, 1997, we will be at 12 Cedar Ave., Battle Creek, Michigan. However, no comma is needed when only the month and year are given—for example, July 1998—and no comma precedes a zip code in an address.

SEMICOLONS

Usually a semicolon is used where a period could have been used; it indicates a major break in the meaning of a sentence.

- Use a semicolon between main clauses not joined by *and, or, nor, but, for,* or *yet.*

We have put in six new burners this past month; none took more than an hour to install.

Tom has found the problem; consequently, we can go ahead as planned.

- Use a semicolon and a comma to replace missing words.

Franklin Pipe installed the plumbing; City Electric, the wiring.

- Use a semicolon to separate items in a series if the items contain commas.

Last month we appraised properties in Tacoma, Washington; Portland, Oregon; and Fairbanks, Alaska.

COLONS

A colon is a promise to the reader. It tells the reader that the next group of words will fulfill what the previous group promised.

- Frequently colons are used after *the following* or *as follows.*

Do these things before you leave: check the office for equipment left running, turn out the lights, lock the door.

- A colon may be used when the second half of the sentence repeats the first half in other words.

We were never deceived: we deceived ourselves.

HYPHENS

- Use a hyphen to link together two or more words that combine to describe the word immediately following.

area-wide survey	fast-moving freight
up-to-the-minute news	far-fetched story
never-say-die attitude	anti-American propaganda

- Use a hyphen in compound nouns. Check a dictionary to be sure because there is no logical pattern to indicate which words are hyphenated and which are not.

sister-in-law	mother-of-pearl
court-martial	go-between
take-out	trade-off

- Use a hyphen between a numeral and its unit of measurement when they modify a noun.

10-cent candy	6-inch section
40-hour week	64-piece puzzle

- Avoid using a hyphen to divide long words at the end of a line of typing.

DASHES

Business writing seldom makes use of dashes. Occasionally a dash may be used for emphasis or to show a sudden interruption in thought.

> The construction ground to a halt six weeks ago—but that is not your problem.

> Can we—dare we—raise the bid?

PARENTHESES

- Use parentheses sparingly.
- Use parentheses to enclose references, dates, and ideas that are only loosely related to the narrative.
- Punctuation marks go inside the parentheses when they apply only to the words inside the parentheses. They go outside when they apply to the whole sentence.

> The research was based on only one issue of *Time* (February 15, 1993).

> Cheryl has found four major accounts since she arrived up there. (No one seems to have told her that it is an impossible territory.)

QUOTATION MARKS

- Quotation marks are needed to indicate an exact transcription of words spoken or passages copied from a printed work. When quoting, the writer must identify the source.

- Quotation marks can signal the reader that a word is being used in an unusual way. If overused, this device can become disruptive and annoying.

- Quotation marks also enclose chapter titles, article titles, or other titles that identify parts of a published work.

- Commas and periods go inside the closing quotation mark; colons and semicolons go outside the closing quotation mark. Question and exclamation marks may go inside or outside depending on whether the mark refers to just the quoted material or to the whole sentence.

ITALICS

In general, italics are used for words and letters that used to be underlined in the age of the typewriter. That is to say, use italics for titles of books and periodicals, foreign words, and words or letters used as terms in sentences. Underlining is no longer appropriate for these purposes.

CHAPTER 7

Documentation

The conclusions in a business report depend on the authority and accuracy of the data and methods used. Providing source information is vital to the persuasiveness of the argument. On the other hand, no one expects a business report to be cluttered with footnotes like a scholarly article. To determine what needs to be documented, the appraiser must exercise careful judgment and recognize that an appraisal is only as good as its sources of information.

Consider first the function of documentation in a report. For the client, it lends authority to the facts and, in some cases, provides a means for the client to investigate the subject further. Source references may also bolster the credibility of the appraisal methods employed. The prime function of documentation, therefore, is to aid and persuade the reader.

Plagiarism is not a primary concern in business reports. While it is often necessary to give credit to an original source or author, especially for copyrighted material, most parts of a report are original or paraphrased writing. It would be absurd to expect citations for every fact, idea, or concept that is not original to the appraiser.

Writers should be sensitive to the real purpose of documentation and to the concerns of the reader. Pity the poor reader who is lured to the bottom of a page simply to find a footnote saying *Ibid.* or *op cit.,* scholarly abbreviations that are not appropriate in business reports.

Most business writers find it more efficient and less disruptive to provide source information in the text, rather than in a footnote. When in-text references are used, a full bibliography giving complete information on each source should be provided at the end of the report. An abbreviated citation in the text supported by a full reference in the bibliography should satisfy most clients. Using standard footnotes is also acceptable if the writer prefers.

The following sections provide an overview of bibliographical form and embedded textual notes. For a complete discussion, consult *The Chicago Manual of Style,* published by the University of Chicago Press, or any other good style manual. Authorities may differ regarding exact punctuation and other niceties involved in creating a bibliography, but all advocate providing the reader with the required information in a logical, consistent style.

BIBLIOGRAPHY

A bibliography is an alphabetized list of sources. Each source entry in the list consists of three parts and each part answers a different question:

1. Who wrote it?
2. What is the exact title of the work?
3. Where can I find it?

This three-part structure is the same for books, periodicals, and virtually all citations. Remember that the proper place to find information for the bibliography is on the title page, not the book's cover.

- *Who wrote it?* For alphabetizing purposes, put the author's last name first. If the work has more than one author, reverse only the first author's name and list the others in order. If the work has no author listed, omit this first part and begin the entry with the title.

- *What is the title of the work?* Write the exact title found on the title page. Use italics for book titles and quotations marks for article titles. If the source is an interview, simple write "Interview." For books, provide the edition number only if the book is not the first edition; ignore the printing number (first printing, second printing, etc.). Page numbers change between editions, but not between printings.

- *Where can I find it?* Provide the reader with enough information to find a copy of the work cited. The required information varies depending on the source. Books require 1) city of publication (include the state only if the city is obscure), 2) publisher's name, and 3) date of this edition. For example,

  Los Angeles: Bantam, 1996

  Articles in journals or periodicals require 1) the name of the journal or periodical in italics, 2) date of the issue, and 3) beginning and ending page numbers of the article. For example,

  The Appraisal Journal, Spring 1997, pp. 347-362.

  For other types of sources, provide enough information for the reader to verify the source, if needed. For interviews this could be the city and date of the interview. The form of the citation is not as important as its content.

A sample of the three-part entries in a bibliography follows. Notice the indentation, which is designed to highlight the alphabetized order of the entries.

The Appraisal of Real Estate. 11th ed. Chicago: Appraisal Institute, 1996.

Fiore, Nicholas J. "Valuing Intangibles." *Journal of Accountancy* (September 1986): 12.

Jones, Thomas. Interview. Denver: August 12, 1997.

Keating, David Michael. *The Valuation of Wetlands.* Chicago: Appraisal Institute, 1995.

Pratt, Shannon P., Robert F. Reilly, and Robert P. Schweihs. *Valuing Small Businesses and Professional Practices.* 2nd ed. Homewood, IL : Business One Irwin, 1993.

NOTES AND FOOTNOTES

Textual notes and citations, which appear in the text and not at the bottom of the page, depend on the bibliography to provide complete source information. Consequently, they are abbreviated references providing only the name of the source (author's last name or a shortened title) and the page number. For example, (Horsman, p. 55) or (*Valuation of a Dental Practice*, p. 103). Placing these citations in parentheses after a quotation or fact provides a quick and easy reference without forcing the reader to stop and look for a footnote.

Informational footnotes, as opposed to source notes, do have a place in valuation reports. They are used to provide explanations of numbers or facts in tables and other exhibits, and they can occasionally explain or support information in the text.

CHAPTER 8

Editing and Proofreading

Editing and proofreading are the final steps in the appraisal process. After days or weeks of research, analysis, and thought working out an appraisal problem, most appraisers are striving to meet a deadline and may be tempted to skip these final steps. Nevertheless, editing and proofreading are crucial to successful reports and are the mark of true professionalism. By taking the time to edit and proofread a report, appraisers can avoid much frustration and potential embarrassment.

EDITING THE REPORT.

The editing part of the writing process technically begins after the first draft is written. Most writers, however, find that they edit as they write. Nevertheless, it is very important to allow time to consider the report as a whole after the first draft is written. In the editing process, the writer has two concerns: Do the logic, content, and argument adequately address the issues involved and support the appraiser's conclusions? and Does the language express the writer's meaning exactly?

Published writers depend on expert editors to consider these issues. A professional editor has the objectivity to view the writing without bias; the writer is usually too close to the work to see it objectively. Unfortunately, appraisers seldom have the luxury of a professional editor.

On the other hand, the rather standardized format of a typical appraisal report usually ensures that all major steps in the appraisal process are covered, at least in a general way. Consequently, it is not the omission, but the adequacy of each section that is in question. For example, is the description and analysis of the subject's neighborhood adequate and does it lead directly to the issues of concern in this appraisal?

To assess the report objectively, the writer needs to view the report as the client or an opposing attorney would. Some points to consider are

- Have all the client's questions and concerns been adequately addressed?

- Do the arguments, explanations, and factual information presented cover the subject fully?
- Is everything truly relevant and pertinent to the issues at hand, or should some sections be eliminated or condensed?
- Is the report consistent throughout? Have all changes or revisions been carried through to all the sections of the report?

The second concern in the editing process is the appropriateness of the language and the wording of the sentences and paragraphs. This handbook has addressed the issues of clarity, word choice, grammar, punctuation, and style, all of which apply to the editing process. In reviewing their reports, writers may ask themselves these questions:

- Are the paragraphs well structured with clearly stated central ideas, or is the main idea buried in the middle of a long paragraph?
- Is the argument expressed passively or is it in the active voice?
- Is there unnecessary verbiage in sentences?
- Is any jargon or technical terminology explained for lay readers?
- Are judgments and conclusions hedged or qualified unnecessarily?
- Are acronyms used liberally and presented without explanation? This can confuse the client.
- Are there problems in grammar or word choice?

In some cases it may be beneficial to have a colleague read and critique the report. He or she may find problems that the author has missed.

PROOFREADING AND CHECKING THE FINAL DRAFT.

Proofreading assures accuracy and correctness so the finished report reflects the careful professionalism that went into the appraisal assignment. Remember that it is the appraiser's signature that appears on the final report.

Some final instructions for the report writer follow.

- Use the spellcheck function on your computer, but don't rely on it totally. It misses many misspellings and misused words.
- Check all numbers to uncover errors in transcription and in calculations.
- Check to be sure that all tables and exhibits are properly titled and/or numbered.
- Be sure the formatting is correct and consistent.
- Make sure that all promised sections or exhibits are included.
- Check the accuracy of any cross-references.

Finally, always check the spelling of the client's name.

CONCLUSION

As every appraiser knows, creating effective appraisal reports is an arduous task, but it is not an insurmountable one. Report writers must keep the primary goal in mind, which is to communicate the data and analysis clearly, concisely, and simply. The reader knows less about the subject than the appraiser does, so the writing must be viewed from the reader's perspective. Logical presentation and a pleasing, reader-friendly format encourage clients to read appraisal reports in depth.

While the appraisal analysis remains objective and unbiased, the report must advocate for the appraiser's conclusions about use and value. To be convincing, the writer must lead the reader through the analysis purposefully and fully reveal the reasons that support each conclusion. Although the final estimate of value is an opinion, it is not plucked out of thin air. Rather, the facts gathered from the market dictate the conclusions, so a well-written report concludes with a sense of inevitability.

The effectiveness of any report is subtly weakened by careless writing errors. This handbook has covered many of the most common writing concerns encountered in the appraisal profession. Despite the hours of research and analysis that go into an appraisal, the language of the report will ultimately determine its success.

Over the years an appraiser's collection of completed appraisals grows and stands as a permanent record of his or her professional career. For most appraisers, these collected works reveal continual changes in format and style. These changes are good insofar as they represent a constant effort to improve the appraiser's work product and meet the changing demands of a dynamic profession. Appraisers who are concerned with creating clear, straightforward reports should take advantage of every opportunity to achieve this lofty goal.